C000281630

Trams, Trolleybuses & Recoll
1958 Part 1 January to Ju

Henry Conn

© Henry Conn 2022

All rights reserved. No part of this publication may be reproduced, stored in a retrieval system or transmitted, in any form or by any means, electronic, mechanical, photocopying, recording or otherwise, without prior permission in writing from Silver Link Books, Mortons Media Group Ltd.

First published in 2022

British Library Cataloguing in Publication Data

A catalogue record for this book is available from the British Library.

ISBN 978 1 85794 587 4

Silver Link Books
Mortons Media Group Limited
Media Centre
Morton Way
Horncastle
LN9 6JR
Tel/Fax: 01507 529535

email: sohara@mortons.co.uk
Website: www.nostalgiacollection.com

Printed and bound in the Czech Republic

Title page: **LEEDS** This view of Feltham 515 working route 20 was taken at the Selby Road railway bridge on 13 June 1958. Appleyard of Leeds Ltd, at the junction of North Street with Sheepscar Street South, was started by John Ernest Appleyard, who opened his first business on Park Row in 1919. The North Street garage opened in October 1927. *David Clarke*

Contents

Acknowledgements

I would like to express my sincere thanks to David and John Clarke for allowing continuing and much appreciated access to their wonderful collection of negatives and slides. All the portraits in this book come from their 1958 collection, and all, bar one, have never been published before.

Introduction

This book is a companion to *Buses, Coaches, Trolleybuses, Trams & Recollections*, No 60 in the series, and *Trams and Trolleybuses 1958 Part 2* No 130 in the series which also covered the year 1958 and were published by Silver Link in 2016 and 2021. This book concentrates on the trams of Glasgow, Leeds and Sheffield and the trolleybuses of London through the travels of brothers David and John Clarke. In these views taken between 15 January and 25 June, we see a multitude of locations, either no longer existing or changed beyond recognition – quiet roads with little traffic, the period cars and lorries, the fashions, the advertisements of long-lost products, the shops, the buildings and the churches.

Enjoy the nostalgia!

SHEFFIELD The first view taken in 1958 was on 15 January, and this is Sheffield Standard No 72. The car alongside is an Austin A40/A50 Cambridge; these were produced in goodly numbers between 1954 and 1957. *David Clarke*

LEEDS On Hunslet Road on 16 January, working a service 25 to Hunslet, is Horsfield tram No 213. The Austin K8 van belongs to Mason, Pork Butchers of Leeds. *David Clarke*

LEEDS On the left of this view is the Golden Lion Hotel, and having just gone under the Leeds Freedom Bridge on Lower Briggate is Feltham No 538, also on 16 January. The Land Rover is a Series 1 produced between 1948 and 1958. *David Clarke*

LEEDS The weather has taken a turn for the worse in this view of Horsfield No 192 heading for Briggate on 19 January. *David Clarke*

LONDON Route 679 ran between Waltham Cross and Smithfield via Edmonton and Finsbury Park route and, apart from a small number of early weekday journeys operated by Highgate, was solely the domain of Edmonton depot. In Highbury on 31 March, heading for Smithfield, is K1 No 1171 (EXV 171). *John Clarke*

LONDON Working route 611 from Moorgate to Highgate Village in Highbury on 31 March is J3 No 1040 (EXV 40). Route 611 ascended and descended Highgate Hill and only trolleybuses with coasting or run-back brakes were allowed on the hill. The two-door estate prominent in this view is an Austin A30. *John Clarke*

LONDON On the same day at the same location, but looking in the opposite direction, heading for Moorgate working route 611 is L1 No 1357 (EXV 357). In the background is an Austin A30 and a very early Reliant Regal convertible, which was produced between 1956 and 1958. *John Clarke*

SHEFFIELD This view of Roberts car No 504 was taken in Prince of Wales Road, with the Darnall railway bridge in the background, on 10 April. No 504 is heading towards Elm Tree, Intake. The Standard motor car appears to have become impatient and is overtaking both the tram car and another car. *David Clarke*

Left: **LEEDS** This view was taken on Great Wilson Street on 14 April. This street was home to Hurst & Woodhead, timber merchants, and Spensall Engineering Co Ltd. Working a service 25 to Hunslet is Horsfield No 154. *David Clarke*

Right: **LEEDS** On Hunslet Road on the same day is Horsfield No 177 working a Middleton Circular; it is fairly obvious that it is quite a warm day as the children are wearing summer skirts and shirts, yet the men are still going around with their flat caps and the ladies are still wearing their long raincoats. *David Clarke*

Left: **LEEDS** At the junction of Neville Street and Sovereign Street on 23 April working a route 25 to Hunslet is Horsfield No 195. Poking its nose out of Little Neville Street is a Rover 75 and behind the tram is a Bedford lorry. *David Clarke*

Right: **LEEDS** At the junction of Meadow Land, Dewsbury Road and Victoria Road on the same day, working a Middleton Circular, is Feltham No 515. The car is a Leeds-registered Vauxhall Victor, and this example is relatively new as the Victor was only launched in February 1957; I remember vividly the car's three-speed column gear change. *David Clarke*

Left: **LEEDS** At the junction of Hunslet Lane and Waterloo Street, also on 23 April, is Feltham No 587; this tram was renumbered to 561 in February 1959 and was sold to Standish, a demolition contractor of South Accommodation, Leeds, in March 1959. The car is an Austin A40 Somerset; I remember my uncle having one of these, with really plush leather seats and a column change. *David Clarke*

Right: **LEEDS** On 28 April at the junction of Hunslet Lane and Great Wilson Street, also working a Middleton Circular, is Feltham No 542. The bus is Samuel Ledgard's No D281 (HGF 958), a Park Royal-bodied Daimler CWA6 new to London Transport in 1946 and acquired via North of Leeds. *David Clarke*

May

LEEDS On 7 May David Clarke took part in a tour of the Leeds tramway system, and this view was taken at Roundhay layby. The Leeds tram used for the tour was Feltham No 589 and this view was taken at 2.43 in the afternoon. I can assure you that, having seen all the views taken on that day, weather-wise this was the best! *David Clarke*

LEEDS At the sub-station working route 20 to Halton on 20 May is Feltham No 528, which was originally 539 but had been renumbered in August 1957. The tram remained in stock at the end of tramway operation, and was sold to Hinchcliffe of Leeds and broken up at Swinegate depot by February 1960. *David Clarke*

LEEDS tram routes 12, 18, 20 and 26 were linked so that cars worked Crossgates-18-12-26-20-26-12-18-Crossgates. These linkages gave convenient cross-city workings for most routes. At Crossgates on 23 May is Feltham No 557, which was renumbered 564 in February 1959 and withdrawn two months later. *David Clarke*

LEEDS At 10.30 on the morning of 23 May this is Feltham No 529 climbing Halton Hill. The No 1 single on this day was *Who's Sorry Now* by Connie Francis. *David Clarke*

LEEDS The next five pictures were taken in Leeds on 13 June. On York Road at the junction with Watson Road is Feltham 505 working route 18 to Crossgates. Another of the renumbered Felthams, this tram was originally 520, receiving its new number in August 1957, and was in stock on the last day of tramway working in Leeds. *David Clarke*

LEEDS The first 50 trams acquired by Leeds from London Transport Executive entered service in the city between October 1950 and August 1951. Working route 12 on Crossgates Road is Feltham No 525. *David Clarke*

Left: **LEEDS** Photographed at 10.55 on that June morning heading for Crossgates is Feltham No 515 on York Road at its junction with Gipton Approach. *David Clarke*

Below: **LEEDS** Also seen on York Road a little later at 11.24, this time at the junction with Freehold Street and Garbutt Street, on route 20 to South Accommodation Road is Feltham No 519. *David Clarke*

LEEDS At the substation at 2.31pm and working the route 12 Middleton Circular is Brush-built Horsfield No 199. Working in the opposite direction and indicating Crossgates on route 18 is Feltham No 536. *David Clarke*

LEEDS Quarry Hill flats, when built in 1938, were considered state-of-the-art living – no more outside toilets in back yards for the tenants – and replaced much of the old housing stock demolished during the widespread slum clearances in the city. The imposing flats fell into a state of decay and were demolished in 1978. They were made famous as the location for the 1970s sitcom *Queenie's Castle* featuring Diana Dors. With the flats providing a backdrop, Feltham No 514 is exiting Marsh Lane into York Road at 10.20am on 17 June. *David Clarke*

Left: **LEEDS** Passing Leeds bus station at 9.13am on 18 June is Feltham No 529; several Leeds tram services passed the bus station but did not enter. The former London Feltham trams had been purchased at a price of £500 each, and of the 90 acquired at least seven did not enter service with Leeds. The cost of overhaul before entry into service in the city was approximately £300 per tram. *David Clarke*

Below left: **LEEDS** The next four views are dated 18 June. On Roundhay Road at its junction with Roseville Road this is Horsfield 191 on route 3 to Moortown. The car disappearing to the right is a Vauxhall Cresta. *David Clarke*

Below: **LEEDS** At Roundhay Park Gates are Horsfields Nos 189 and 240. It was here on 4 September 1952 that a tram car careered driverless all the way from the Park Gates to the Oakwood parade of shops. The tram smashed into a city-bound tram before mounting the pavement. The driver had left the tram without applying the parking brake and the conductor, who should have applied the emergency brake, jumped off in panic. At Oakwood the driver and conductor of the other tram were knocked unconscious as the tram was shunted from the stop at high speed. At Gipton Wood the tram was stopped by a passenger, who jumped on and applied the emergency brake. *David Clarke*

Left: **LEEDS** At the junction of Meadow Lane, to the left, and Bridge End this is Feltham tram No 549. Forming a fair proportion of the backdrop to this view is the British Waterways offices, which are now modern flats. *David Clarke*

Below left: **LEEDS** At Burton Road at 3.09 in the afternoon, working route 12, is Feltham No 538. This tram survived until the end of the Leeds tramway system and was scrapped at Swinegate depot in January 1960. *David Clarke*

Below: **SHEFFIELD** Works car No 330 was one of several cars from other cities purchased by Sheffield during the Second World War to maintain public services needed to cater for the extra traffic associated with increased industrial production and the lack of buses. Originally a double-deck car, No 330 lost the top deck when withdrawn after the war to take up duties as a works car. This view was taken on 19 June at Snig Hill. *John Clarke*

Right: **SHEFFIELD** The next nine pictures were taken in Sheffield on 19 June. No 330 is seen again outside Tenter Street depot; survived until the end of tramway operations in Sheffield and is now in preservation at Crich. Following No 330 is an Austin K8 van, which was produced between 1947 and 1954. *John Clarke*

Below: **SHEFFIELD** Between 1936 and 1939 the Queens Road Works built cars that were known as the 'domed-roof' class. Seen at the works is Standard domed-roof car No 288, with no destination blinds set, indicating that it is out of service. *John Clarke*

Below right: **SHEFFIELD** On Queens Road is Standard domed-roof No 270, which was built in 1937; note the man hanging on in the back of the Electricity Service lorry. *John Clarke*

Above left: **SHEFFIELD** In the fully lined-out old livery of Prussian blue and cream and with the large numerals associated with the old livery, this is Standard car No 63. The scene is a very quiet High Street, and No 63 is indicating a journey to Owlerton. *John Clarke*

Above: **SHEFFIELD** Passing the Grand Hotel on Leopold Street is Standard No 170. The Grand occupied all of the Fountain Precinct site opposite the bottom side of the City Hall, Orchard Lane and that part of Leopold Street up to what is bow the Yorkshire Building Society. It was Sheffield's most prestigious hotel, 'the' place to stay in Sheffield and very much a place for the stars to stop over when they had played the Sheffield venues. The Grand Hotel was demolished in 1973 to make way for the Fountain Precinct. *John Clarke*

Left: **SHEFFIELD** The Cole brothers, John and Thomas, opened a silk mercer and hosier business at 4 Fargate, Sheffield, in 1847. Their brother Skelton almost immediately joined them in the business, which grew rapidly, purchasing stores along Fargate and round into Church Street. The business grew so much that in 1869 a rebuild of the stores was commissioned with a new frontage and an extra two storeys. With the Cole Brothers store as a backdrop, this is Standard car No 160, also still in the old fully lined-out livery. *John Clarke*

Above: **SHEFFIELD** Passing C&A on High Street, which is not looking too busy on this June day, is Standard No 197 indicating Weedon Street, Tinsley. C&A in Sheffield lasted until January 2001; Primark announced the acquisition of the Sheffield building on 19 September 2000. *John Clarke*

Above right: **SHEFFIELD** This is Fitzalan Square, with the Elephant Inn on the right, on the corner where Norfolk Street entered the square. The pub closed in the late 1960s and later became a branch of Halfords, then a charity shop. Car No 69 is a Standard car built in 1930, and car No 271 beyond it is a Standard domed-roof car. *John Clarke*

Right: **SHEFFIELD** The Yorkshire Penny Bank building originally housed the Post Office and was opened in 1872; the Penny Bank moved into the building in May 1926. The 'Penny' was dropped in 1959 when it became simply the Yorkshire Bank. This was a very busy junction requiring police control, and Standard domed-roof car No 260 appears to have been given the go-ahead. The bus behind No 260 is one of the Roe-bodied Leyland PD2/12s that had entered service in 1957. *John Clarke*

Left: **LEEDS** The next 24 views of Leeds trams were taken on 20 June. This is Feltham No 509 near Temple Newsam; it was one of the 90 vehicles acquired from London Transport in 1950, and remained in the Leeds fleet until July 1959, when it was sold to George Cohen Ltd for scrapping. *John Clarke*

Below left: **LEEDS** Manfield, one of whose shoe shops is seen in the background in this view at Briggate, was founded in the 1840s and by 1851 employed 200 people in Northampton. By 1950 Manfield had 92 branches in the UK and Ireland. However, in 1956 the business was acquired by Sears and became part of the British Shoe Corporation; latterly Manfield was integrated with Saxone. Horsfield cars Nos 219 and 221 exchanged their numbers in December 1957, and this is the renumbered 221; it had been new in 1931 and was sold for scrap in June 1959. *John Clarke*

Below: **LEEDS** Passing Lewis's store on The Headrow is Horsfield No 199, built by Brush in 1931. The store was opened in September 1932 at a cost of around £750,000; it comprised 157 departments from which everything could be purchased, from a theatre ticket to a permanent wave, a pound of sausages to a suite of furniture. Initially there was a permanent staff of about 1,000, of whom 850 were women and girls. In its first year of working the store showed a clear profit. At the outset only two basement floors and two ground floors were in operation, but in 1936 the third floor was finished, and 1938 saw further additions. Following the demise of the company, the Leeds store became a branch of Allders in the 1990s, and now houses branches of TK Maxx, Argos and Sainsbury's, among others. *John Clarke*

1958 Happenings (1)

January
The European Economic Community is founded

Sputnik 1, launched in October 1957, falls to Earth

The first successful US satellite, Explorer 1, is launched into orbit.

February
Egypt and Syria unite to form the United Arab Republic, and Gamal Nasser becomes first President

A hydrogen bomb is lost in the waters off Georgia, USA

Seven Manchester United footballers are among 21 people killed in Munich air disaster

Pope Pius XII declares St Clare the patron saint of television

Bertrand Russell launches the Campaign for Nuclear Disarmament

March
British and Commonwealth team led by Sir Vivian Fuchs completes first overland crossing of Antarctic, using Snowcat caterpillar tractors and dogsled teams

The US Army launches Explorer 3

The Bridge on the River Kwai wins seven awards at the 30th Academy Awards

Nikita Khrushchev becomes Premier of the Soviet Union

April
BBC Radiophonic Workshop is established

In Cuba, Castro's revolutionary army begins attacks on Havana

LEEDS To the right of this view in Vicar Lane is Heatons, a tailoring company that moved into the building around 1914 and started business in 1916, closing down in the 1970s. Heading for Briggate is Horsfield car No 171, another Brush-built car from 1931. Also on the right is a Standard Vanguard Phase III, and also in view are a couple of Austin A30s, a Ford and a Rover on the extreme left. *John Clarke*

LEEDS At North Street and Brunswick Street, with Heatons building to the left, working route 3 to Harehills is numerically the last of the Brush-bodied Horsfields, car No 254, which entered service in 1932. *John Clarke*

Right: **LEEDS** On the left of this view is the Midland Bank building on North Street, and passing it is Horsfield car No 154, one of four prototypes built by Leeds City Transport in 1930. Note the two cars to the right, both Vauxhall Cresta Es, the one fully in view having a local Leeds registration number and probably new in 1957. *John Clarke*

Above: **LEEDS** Look at the lovely array of local shops in this view taken in North Street, a very rare sight now. Working route 3 is Brush-built Horsfield No 156, new in 1951, which survived until the end of the tramway system in Leeds on 7 November 1959 and was sold to Cohen's for scrap in January 1960. *John Clarke*

Right: **LEEDS** At Sheepscar, note the movement of the Ford in the centre of the picture, which seems to me to be on the wrong side of the road with cars and buses heading towards it from all directions! Leaving the scene of possible trouble is Brush-bodied Horsfield car No 162, new in 1931. *John Clarke*

LEEDS The Horsfield trams were named after the new manager of the Leeds system, Mr R. L. Horsfield, who arrived in 1928 and died in 1931. They were also called 'Showboats'. Four prototype cars were built by Leeds City Transport in 1930, Nos 151-154, and 100 similar cars, Nos 155-254, were ordered from Brush for delivery in 1931. This is No 196 at Sheepscar. The rider of the scooter is not wearing a safety helmet – not very clever even in the late 1950s! *John Clarke*

LEEDS On Zetland Street working route 3, a Briggate circular to Roundhay and Moortown, is Brush-built Horsfield car No 166. Either being passed by or passing No 166 is Leeds No 677 (PUA 677), a Roe-bodied AEC Regent III new in 1952. *John Clarke*

1958 Happenings (2)

April *continued*
   First CND protest march from Hyde Park to Aldermaston
   Satellite Sputnik 2 disintegrates in space after several orbits
   King of Belgium opens World's Fair, Expo 58, in Brussels

May
   Actor-singer Paul Robeson sells out two one-man concerts at Carnegie Hall, but is seldom seen in public in the US again
   Military coup in Algeria
   Soviet Union launches Sputnik 3
   Cuban government launches counter-offensive against Castro's rebels
   Real Madrid win European Cup

June
   Charles de Gaulle is brought out of retirement to lead France by decree for six months
   Pizza Hut is founded
   World's last fully rigged sailing ship trading under sail alone, built in 1887, sinks
   Brazil wins football World Cup

July
   Earthquake in Alaska causes landslide and mega-tsunami, with waves reaching 525m (1,722ft)
   First parking meters installed in UK
   Revolution in Iraq – King Faisal killed, and Abdul Qassim assumes power
   5,000 US Marines land in Beirut, Lebanon, to protect pro-Western government there

Above: **LEEDS** This view was taken on Harehills Road. Note the advertisement on the side of Horsfield No 254. Jesse Stephenson opened his first grocery shop in 1903; he soon introduced a bakery and also a dividend system, and in 1923 he built a large new bakery on the site in New Street, Farsley, later to be used as a retail outlet. 'Sunshine Bread' baked at this site became a household word throughout the West Riding. *John Clarke*

Above right: **LEEDS** To the left of this view is The Clock Cinema, at the junction of Roundhay Road and Easterly Road. It was built for West Leeds Entertainments and opened on 21 November 1938; it closed on 28 February 1976. Passing The Clock is Brush-built Horsfield No 254. The Leeds bus is No 473 (MUG 473), a Roe-bodied AEC Regent III new in 1949. *John Clarke*

Right: **LEEDS** Working route 3 on the Harehills spur is Leeds City Transport-built Horsfield prototype No 154. *John Clarke*

Above: **LEEDS** The Horsfields were said to be the most popular of the Leeds cars and many remained in operation until the end of the city's tram system. When new they featured flush side panels, two-and-one seating and air brakes. At Gledhow Wood Road is Brush-built No 171, which featured on the last day of Leeds tramcars and was specially numbered 8 for the final day. *John Clarke*

Above right: **LEEDS** On Ravenscar Avenue is Brush-bodied Horsfield No 166. The Stylo advert on the tram's front was a popular tramcar feature. Stylo was a family-run shoe business that had started in 1935 and, having grown to 150 outlets in 1964, purchased W. Barratt & Co and merged in Bradford, trading under the better-known trade name of Barratts. *John Clarke*

Right: **LEEDS** This is the large Oakwood Clock at the bottom end of Roundhay Park, built in 1904 by Potts of Leeds to the design of Leeming & Leeming. It was first designed as the centrepiece of Kirkgate market, but after the design of the market was revised the clock was placed at Oakwood instead. The tram in this view is one of the four Leeds-built Horsfield trams, No 154. *John Clarke*

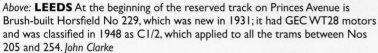

Above: **LEEDS** At the beginning of the reserved track on Princes Avenue is Brush-built Horsfield No 229, which was new in 1931; it had GEC WT28 motors and was classified in 1948 as C1/2, which applied to all the trams between Nos 205 and 254. *John Clarke*

Above right: **LEEDS** The Leeds tramway system was the key factor in the development of Roundhay as a suburb and the popularity of the park at weekends and holidays for the city's residents. At the first crossover at Roundhay Park is Horsfield No 166. *John Clarke*

Right: **LEEDS** At the second crossover at Roundhay Park is No 154, one of the Leeds City Tramways-built Horsfield prototypes. Indicating Dewsbury Road on route 2 is bus No 850 (XUM 850), a Roe-bodied AEC Regent V new in 1957, which was one of a batch of 55 all of which had 7ft 6in-wide bodywork. *John Clarke*

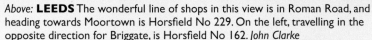

Above: **LEEDS** The wonderful line of shops in this view is in Roman Road, and heading towards Moortown is Horsfield No 229. On the left, travelling in the opposite direction for Briggate, is Horsfield No 162. *John Clarke*

Above right: **LEEDS** In Moor Allerton Avenue is Horsfield No 171. Noteworthy is the lack of traffic – one tram, one bus and two cars. The nearest car is a Leeds-registered Austin A30; it is recognisable as the A30 had a smaller rear window than the A35 and had trafficators, which popped out from the B pillar. *John Clarke*

Right: **LEEDS** With the Walker & Hall showroom at Briggate in the background, this is Feltham No 568 working the Middleton Circular route. A total of 15 Felthams purchased in 1950 did not enter service until 1955 and 1956, No 568 being one of them. The cars in view are the rear of a Ford Consul, and on the other side of the road a Ford Anglia and an Austin A30 van. *John Clarke*

Above: **LEEDS** At Bishopgate, with Leeds station in the background, is Horsfield No 215 working route 25 to Hunslet. *John Clarke*

Above right: **LEEDS** The last of the 20 June photographs shows Neville Street, with Little Neville Street to the left and Sovereign Street to the right, and Leeds City-built Horsfield prototype No 153. The large car on the left might be a Humber, then a Morris pick-up, a Volkswagen Beetle and an A30 van. The bus following No 153 is an MCCW-bodied Daimler CVG6 new in 1956. *John Clarke*

Right: **LEEDS** At the junction of Great Wilton Street and Hunslet Lane on 21 June is Horsfield No 222. There are two Morris Minor Travellers in this view, with between them an early production Bedford CA van. *John Clarke*

Above: **LEEDS** Brush-built Horsfield car No 192 is passing the Clarendon on the corner of Victoria Road and Water Lane. The van following it is an Austin A40 van and the lorry carrying the milk churns is I think a Commer. *John Clarke*

Above right: **GLASGOW** is our next destination, and the next 23 views were all taken on 23 June. At 9.40am on Paisley Road working route 4 to Springburn is No 301, a Standard round-dash car that was originally a double-deck open-balcony tram when built in 1909 and was modernised with a closed top deck in the late 1920s. Route 4 was withdrawn on 6 September 1958 and replaced by bus service 53. On at the Imperial is *The Wild Party*, a 1956 film with Anthony Quinn, and *Sitting Bull*, a 1954 film with Dale Robertson. *John Clarke*

Right: **GLASGOW** Originally Cessnock Dock, Prince's Dock was completed in 1897 and was renamed in honour of the Duke of York, who performed the opening ceremony. The dock contained 35 acres of water space, and its bustling quays were generously equipped with two-storey warehouses, cranes, coal hoists and a maze of railway sidings. About to pass an entrance to Prince's Dock at 10.03am is No 137, which was originally a rear-entrance front-exit car fitted with swivel chairs in the upper saloon, but was later converted to normal seating. *John Clarke*

Above: **GLASGOW** At Maxwell Street in Pollokshaws at 10.14am are Cunarders Nos 1305 and 1307, both new in 1939. The car in view to the right is a Standard Ten, which was produced between 1954 and 1960. *David Clarke*

Above right: **GLASGOW** Cunarder No 1305 is at Shawlands Cross, with Pollokshaws Road stretching ahead, Kilmarnock Road leading off to the left and Moss-side Road out of view to the right. The church on the corner of Moss-side and Pollokshaws Road was the United Free Church, now Shawlands Cross Church, designed by Miller & Black and built 1900-03. It was built of silver-grey sandstone and an octagonal timber bell turret was erected in place of a tower. Further down Pollokshaws Road at No 1120, and just visible behind the United Free Church, is Shawlands Old Parish Church; this was designed by John A. Campbell of John Burnet, Son & Campbell and built between 1885 and 1889. The facade fronting the Cross was modelled on Dunblane Cathedral and the three stained-glass windows that remain today were completed by Douglas Hamilton in 1950 as a war memorial. *David Clarke*

Right: **GLASGOW** At the Merrylee terminus of route 31 is Standard hex-dash No 231. The last car on route 31 departed from Union Street for Lambhill at 11.15pm on 5 December 1959 and there was no replacement bus service. *David Clarke*

Above: **GLASGOW** Working route 22 on Paisley Road between Crookston and Lambhill is No 1341, a Cunarder new in 1950. Route 22 was withdrawn on 22 November 1958 and replaced by bus service 54. Following the tram is a Western SMT ECW-bodied Bristol LD, and the car is an Austin 7. *John Clarke*

Above right: **GLASGOW** On Paisley Road at its junction with Corkerhill Road, also working route 22, is No 71, a Standard hex-dash car; route 22 cars were allocated from either Possilpark or Govan depots. *John Clarke*

Right: **GLASGOW** At Bellahouston Park on Paisley Road heading for Crookston on route 22 is No 303, a Standard round-dash car. The car prominently in view is a Bristol-registered Austin A40, and the car to the right of the tram is a Standard Vanguard Phase 1 saloon. *John Clarke*

Above: **GLASGOW** Also at Bellahouston Park, No 359, a Standard round-dash car, is working route 3 to the University from Mosspark via Charing Cross. Route 3 was withdrawn on 4 June 1960 and replaced by bus service 59. *John Clarke*

Above right: **GLASGOW** Standard round-dash car No 303 is seen again at Bellahouston Park, working route 22. The van is an Austin K, and just emerging from behind the tram is an Albion lorry, possibly a CX7; Albion lorries and buses were manufactured at Scotstoun in Glasgow and were produced there until 1980 (1972 for complete vehicles). *John Clarke*

Right: **GLASGOW** Cunarder No 1362, new in 1950, is seen on Paisley Road at its junction with Edmiston Drive. Passing the tram is an eight-wheel rigid AEC Mammoth Major, which has an Angus registration. *John Clarke*

Above: **GLASGOW** Working route 32 between Crookston and Springburn or Bishopbriggs on Paisley Road at its junction with Harley Street is Cunarder No 1342, new in 1950. Route 32 was withdrawn on 15 November 1958 and replaced by bus route 25. *John Clarke*

Above right: **GLASGOW** Working route 14 from Arden to the University at Thornliebank Industrial Estate is Standard round-dash car No 413. A new terminus at Arden was opened 4 October 1953 and from 29 September 1956 all the University cars were curtailed at Arden, previously terminating at Cross Stobs. *David Clarke*

Right: **GLASGOW** This view of Coronation No 1164 was taken by David Clarke at Main Street, Thornliebank, at 2.52 in the afternoon; meanwhile at the same time his brother John was taking the next view in Govan. The van is a Morris J, which was produced between 1949 and 1961. *David Clarke*

Above: **GLASGOW** Nearing Govan depot on route 12 is Standard hex-dash car No 70. The car behind it is a Vauxhall Cresta. Note the advert for William Younger's 'Monk' Export Ale, which was produced between 1954 and 1957, and a half-pint would cost you 15d. *John Clarke*

Above right: **GLASGOW** Taken three minutes after the last view is this one of Standard round-dash car No 464 at Main Street, Thornliebank, heading for the route 14 terminus at Arden. *David Clarke*

Right: **GLASGOW** At the junction of Commerce Street and Kingston Street, working route 22 to Crookston, is Standard hex-dash car No 31; the lorry behind is an Austin K4 Loadstar. *John Clarke*

Right: **GLASGOW** On Thornliebank Road near its junction with Burnfield Road is Standard hex-dash car No 234. To the left of the view is, I think, Eastwood Old Cemetery. *David Clarke*

Below: **GLASGOW** The depots providing cars for route 4 were Possilpark and Govan, and the last car ran on 6 September 1958. Crossing the King George V Bridge, which was opened in 1928, is Standard hex-dash car No 102, and the nearest car is a split-screen Morris Minor. *John Clarke*

Below right: **GLASGOW** In Oswald Street we see Cunarder No 1353, which was built in 1950. The bus running behind it, working route 15, is an Alexander-bodied AEC Regent V new in 1955. The walls in the background are overloaded with large paper advertisements. *John Clarke*

Above: **GLASGOW** Due to the tight curves along the route, only Standards were employed on route 12 between Mount Florida and Paisley Road Toll. Approaching roadworks at Linthouse is Standard round-dash car No 643, with a ladies' meeting in the road on the extreme right. *John Clarke*

Above right: **GLASGOW** At Paisley Road Toll on route 12 is Standard round-dash car No 580. To the right of the view is a Nuffield Oxford taxi cab, which was built between 1947 and 1953. Interestingly the Nuffield was assembled in Birmingham, and the one in view has a Birmingham registration number, LOJ 38. Fewer than 2,000 Nuffield taxis were built. *John Clarke*

Right: **GLASGOW** The last view in this sequence, taken at 5.30 in the early evening of 23 June, shows Prince's Docks in the background as heading for Mount Florida and Hampden Park on route 12 is No 13, a Standard hex-dash car. Partially obscured by the pole is a Western SMT Leyland Titan, new in 1957. *John Clarke*

Above: **GLASGOW** The next 19 pictures were taken on the following day, 24 June. On route 6 at 9.33am, travelling from Alexandra Park on a short working to Charing Cross is No 1144, one of the first Coronation cars built in 1937. The small minibus on the right is a Morris LC5, which was produced between 1954 and 1960. *John Clarke*

Above right: **GLASGOW** Four minutes after the previous view was taken by John, David was at the junction of Argyle Street and Oswald Street taking a view of Standard round-dash No 662 working route 9 to Auchenshuggle. *David Clarke*

Right: **GLASGOW** Crossing King George V Bridge is Cunarder No 1362, which was new in 1950. Route 4 would be withdrawn on 6 September 1958, just over ten weeks after this view was taken. *David Clarke*

1958 No 1 Records

January
    Jerry Lee Lewis   *Great Balls of Fire*
    Elvis Presley   *Jailhouse Rock*

February
    Michael Holliday   *The Story of my Life*
    Perry Como   *Magic Moments*

April
    Marvin Rainwater   *Whole Lotta Woman*

May
    Connie Francis   *Who's Sorry Now?*

June
    Vic Damone   *On the Street Where You Live*

July
    Everly Brothers   *All I Have to do is Dream/*
                               Claudette

August
    Kalin Twins   *When*

September
    Connie Francis   *Carolina Moon/Stupid Cupid*

November
    Tommy Edwards   *It's All in the Game*
    Lord Rockingham's XI   *Hoots Mon*

December
    Conway Twitty   *It's Only Make Believe*

Above: **GLASGOW** On the south side of the River Clyde at the junction of Commerce Street and Nelson Street is Standard hex-dash car No 44. *David Clarke*

Left: **GLASGOW** On Morrison Street at its junction with West Street is Cunarder No 1352, new in 1950. The Perthshire-registered A35 van would appear to be very overloaded – and note the horse drawn wagon, loaded I think with coal, at 7s 9d a bag. *David Clarke*

Above: **GLASGOW** On Paisley Road near its junction with Weir Street is Standard round-dash No 929. The plethora of adverts on the gable end of the tenement includes OMO, Monk Export, Creamola Custard, Penguin biscuits, Player's tobacco, McEwan's Export and Bassett's Allsorts; I am not surprised that the top right board is empty – quite a climb to get up there. *David Clarke*

Above right: **GLASGOW** At Corkerhill Road, the Mosspark terminus of route 3, is Standard hex-dash car No 84. The Mosspark terminus had been extended from Mosspark Boulevard to Corkerhill Road on 3 May 1938. *David Clarke*

Right: **GLASGOW** This is Paisley Road West, and David is standing in Lourdes Avenue taking this view of Cunarder No 1346. *David Clarke*

GLASGOW In Cambridge Street, between Baillieston and Maryhill on route 23 is No 1220, a Coronation new in 1938. Strachan's Austin K8 van has a Lanarkshire registration number. *John Clarke*

GLASGOW At the junction of Sauchiehall Street and Cambridge Street working route 1 to Dennistoun is Standard hex-dash car No 53. Reid & Todd Ltd was well known for its excellent leather goods. There a number of 1950s cars in this view including a couple of A30s, a Ford Consul, a Hillman Minx and a Hillman estate. *John Clarke*

GLASGOW At the junction of Hope Street and Renfrew Street, car No 471 on route 22 is, I think, the lesser part of this view — I think the lad crossing the road concentrating on his parcel is what most would look at first. I sincerely hope that this view was taken at a weekend or an evening, otherwise the lad could be in trouble. *John Clarke*

1958 Happenings (3)

July *continued*
> First life peerage created in UK
> US launches Explorer 4
> Queen Elizabeth II gives Prince Charles the title Prince of Wales
> National Aeronautics and Space Administration (NASA) established

August
> Last *Tom and Jerry* cartoon made by Hanna-Barbera — characters not seen again until 1961
> Nuclear-powered submarine USS *Nautilus* is first vessel to cross North Pole under water
> Nabokov's controversial novel Lolita published in USA
> Civil war in China
> US begins nuclear tests over South Atlantic
> Notting Hill race riots

September
> First 'Cod War' begins between UK and Iceland
> Majority in France vote yes to constitution of the Fifth Republic

October
> Guinea declares itself independent from France
> BOAC becomes first airline to fly jet passenger services across the Atlantic, using De Havilland Comets
> Pioneer 1 is first spacecraft launched by newly formed NASA

1958 Arrivals & Departures

Jools Holland	Musician	24 January
Ellen deGeneres	Actress and comedienne	26 January
Mary Chapin Carpenter	Singer	21 February
Nik Kershaw	Singer	1 March
Miranda Richardson	Actress	3 March
Andy Gibb	Singer	5 March
Rik Mayall	Comedian and actor	7 March
Gary Numan	Singer	8 March
Sharon Stone	Actress	10 March
Linda Robson	Actress	13 March
Holly Hunter	Actress	20 March
Gary Oldman	Actor	21 March
Alec Baldwin	Actor	3 April
Peter Capaldi	Actor	14 April
Andie MacDowell	Actress	21 April
Derek Dick ('Fish')	Singer	25 April
Michelle Pfeiffer	Actress	29 April
Catherine Tate	Comedienne and actress	12 May
Paul Whitehouse	Comedian and actor	17 May
Toyah Willcox	Singer and actress	18 May
Paul Weller	Singer/songwriter	25 May
Jennifer Saunders	Comedienne and actress	6 July

Kevin Bacon	Actor	8 July
Pauline Quirke	Actress	8 July
Fiona Shaw	Actress	10 July
Michael Flatley	Dancer	16 July
Kate Bush	Musician	30 July
Bruce Dickinson	Musician	7 August
Madonna Ciccone (Madonna)	Singer and actress	16 August
Belinda Carlisle	Singer	17 August
Tim Burton	Film director	25 August
Michael Jackson	Singer	29 August
Chris Columbus	Film director	10 September
Siobhan Fahey	Singer	10 September
Andrea Bocelli	Tenor	22 September
Irvine Welsh	Author	27 September
Tim Robbins	Actor	16 October
Simon Le Bon	Singer	27 October
Mary Elizabeth Mastrantonio	Actress	17 November
Jamie Lee Curtis	Actress	22 November
Nick Park	Animator	6 December
Alannah Myles	Singer/songwriter	25 December

GLASGOW This is Standard hex-dash car No 28 in Maitland Street on route 4 to Hillington Road. The van beside it is an elderly Fordson E83W. *John Clarke*

Edna Purviance	Actress	(b1895)	11 January
Ernst Heinkel	Aircraft designer and manufacturer	(b1888)	30 January
Christabel Pankhurst	Suffragette	(b 1880)	13 February
Duncan Edwards	Manchester Utd footballer	(b1936)	21 February
Harry Cohn	Film producer	(b1891)	27 February
Mike Todd	Film producer	(b1909)	22 March
W. C. Handy	Blues composer	(b1873)	28 March
Ronald Colman	Actor	(b1891)	19 May
Robert Donat	Actor	(b1905)	9 June
Julia Lennon	Mother of John Lennon	(b1914)	15 July

Harry Warner	Warner Bros studio executive	(b1881)	25 July
Gladys Presley	Mother of Elvis	(b1912)	14 August
Ralph Vaughan Williams	Composer	(b1872)	26 August
Marie Stopes	Birth control pioneer	(b1880)	2 October
Pius XII	Pope	(b1876)	9 October
Tyrone Power	Actor	(b1914)	15 November

GLASGOW Heading for Crookston at Garscube Road is Standard round-dash car No 466. The Grand is showing *The Duke Wore Jeans* starring Tommy Steele and directed by Gerald Thomas, best known for his direction of many of the 'Carry On' films. *John Clarke*

GLASGOW In Dobbies Loan this is Standard hex-dash car No 269. The Bedford O with the Glasgow registration on the right belongs to Mackenzie Partners, while behind No 269 is an Albion artic and a trolleybus. *John Clarke*

GLASGOW On Garscube Road at its junction with Possil Road is Standard round-dash car No 316. This view was taken at 4.16 in the afternoon, and the young lad running must be late getting home. The van on the right is a Morris Minor. *John Clarke*

Above left: **GLASGOW** Being ushered forward by the traffic policeman at the junction of Garscube Road with St Georges Road is Standard round-dash car No 617. Is the British Railways artic behind the tram a Seddon 3-tonner? *John Clarke*

Above: **GLASGOW** On St Georges Road at its junction with Myrtle Street is Standard hex-dash car No 113. On 16 March 1958 the operation of route 16 changed from Possilpark to Partick depot. *John Clarke*

Left: **GLASGOW** At the junction of St Georges Road and Woodland Road is Coronation No 1186, new in 1938. Note the advertisement for Digger Shag in the background; Player's introduced the Digger brand in 1917 and it was an all-Empire leaf tobacco, grown in Rhodesia, Nyasaland, India or Canada. Empire or Commonwealth tobacco had a lower duty tax, so brands that were made with it sold at a lower cost. Digger is no longer produced. *John Clarke*

Above: **GLASGOW** The last view in the city on 24 June was taken at 4.46 in the afternoon on Woodlands Road, and working route 3 between Mosspark and University is Standard hex-dash No 65. On the right is an Austin FX3, which at the date of this picture was in its last year of production, to be replaced by the Austin FX4. *John Clarke*

Above right: **GLASGOW** The next seven views were taken the following day, 25 June. At Shawlands at 9.45 in the morning, working route 8 to Newlands, is Standard round-dash car No 364. The lorry with the milk churns has travelled from Galston in Ayrshire. *John Clarke*

Right: **GLASGOW** At Midday this is Standard round-dash car No 555 at Shieldhall Spur. *David Clarke*

Above: **GLASGOW** Standard hex-dash car No 102 is at Hillington Road and the conductor is just about to change the destination screens. On 11 May 1957 all cars from Springburn terminated at Hillington Road. *David Clarke*

Above left: **GLASGOW** At Elmvale Street in Springburn is Cunarder No 1316, new in 1949. In the background is The Terminus Bar – at one time this marked the very edge of the city's transportation system. The buildings pictured disappeared in the 1970s to make room for lots of big roads and flyovers, leaving this view virtually unrecognisable today. *David Clarke*

Left: **GLASGOW** A nice contrast here between No 1167 on the right, a Coronation new in 1938, and Cunarder No 1367, new in 1950. This view was taken at 1.57 in the afternoon on Springburn Road and Leckethill Street. *David Clarke*